DULL DAYS OF THE 1970s

Dull Days Of The 1970s

Images and words to help you

feel the dullness

Nigel Norman

Braidburn Books

ISBN: 978-1999920432

Published by Braidburn Books

To everyone sitting on a bus in the rain, on a windy station platform, in a lonely house with flies headbutting the window panes, standing ball-less on the wing in a sleet-streaked rugby match, slumped in a worn chair at Granny's as the conversation drones overhead and, particularly, to the entire population of Glenrothes...

...this book is for you.

INTRODUCTION

You might be wondering why I have bothered to compile a book of images of dull days from a decade long gone. "What could possibly be interesting about that, Nigel?" I hear you say. And I would reply, "Well, nothing obviously. The pictures are dull. The literal opposite of interesting." So why do it at all?

For several reasons. Who says a book has to be interesting? I have read a large number of books that were trying to be interesting but were in fact dreadfully dull. It is surely more honest to commit to creating a dull book from the outset. No browsing potential reader could ever claim to be disappointed.

Secondly, I find it ironic that 95% of the snaps that people adorn their virtual lives with are of smiling individuals in joy-filled occasions: by the pool on holiday; a work night out in the pub; a happy meeting of pals. Yet 95% of actual life is utterly ordinary: waiting for a train that's late. Walking to the shops. Being disappointed in the rain. Bathgate. Surely it makes more sense to document the world and one's life in it by recording these moments?

Then there is my own personal feeling on the matter. I was a young child in the 1970s and the most common reminiscence I hear of those days is, "Ah, remember how long and warm the summers were then! 1976 in particular - nothing could touch that year!" And I do remember the hot days of June 1976. I spent most of them flicking rabbit droppings down the hillside near where I lived because all my friends were on holiday. It was dull.

A few years ago, I happened to be browsing through some photography archives when I discovered that quite a few snappers have shared my sensibilities over the decades. I began to curate these images, adding little captions that explained the scene to me; that placed them in the world in their dullness. These images and narratives I now present to you here.

Of course, I don't expect many people will want to actually put down their own good money for such a book, nor read it should some sarcastic relative gift it to them. But that is fine by me.

It keeps things nice and dull.

Nigel Norman
September 2018

The lad holding the polystyrene cups is putting a brave face on it, but you can tell that this was a very dull day. Mud. Waterproofs. Hands jammed in tartan bomber jacket pockets. Dirty hoses. The guy in the shades is looking off to a different scene that he wishes he was in. "I should be over there," he's thinking. "On that yacht with those supermodels. Yet here I am with these coffee-obsessed dullards."

And just like that, our lives are whittled away, one dull day at a time.

The junction of Newton Road, Freeman Road
and Jesmond Park West, Newcastle
1972

This horse has had enough. The greyness of the day
has got to him and he's just jacked it all in. Good
on him. Adding to the deeply dull beauty of this
image is that fact that no one cares. The horse's
cart is about to shed its load; no one cares. The
kerb is going to jigger that axle; no one cares. In a
moment the horse is going to leave the scene entirely
in a search for thistles on the dog-dirt encrusted
wasteground off to the right. No. One. Cares.

There isn't even anyone around who *could* care.

Tube, London
1970

Is it possible to infer from a photograph of an interior whether
the day outside was dull? Yes, I believe that on occasion it is,
and Exhibit A in my case is this image. The Tube travellers all
have that air of resignation that settles on us when deep grey
clouds have settled over the country. There is no hope at all
that any amusement will be forthcoming today. Also, you can see
that everyone in this car is a local; well, a Londoner. There
are no tourists in their brightly coloured clothes to cheer the
scene with some wanderlust-inspired optimism. However, I don't
believe that this is a wet day - there are no dripping umbrellas
or damp shoes. Nor is it midwinter; there are no heavy coats and
one man has a sleeve rolled up. I'd say this is was taken around
11.50 am on a Thursday that started off sunny but clouded over
just after breakfast.

Marston Moor, England
9 April 1977

I went on a canal boat holiday once. It was me and my girlfriend and three of my mates. Don't quite remember why that seemed like a good idea. We started near Birmingham. There was a lot of congestion on the drive there. We picked up the boat in a muddy yard beside a marina. They're really very small. Headed north, motor chugging. I thought it would be peaceful and relaxing. And it was, for about 3 hours. Then it got dull. Just the canal and rain, in the Midlands. We ended up drinking a lot. One day my friend Andy started drinking at 9.30am it was so dull. Another day we moored at a pub. Had a few ales. Later, I lay down on top of the boat with my legs dangling off the side. Maybe I was looking at the stars. Next thing I know, I woke up underwater. Everyone was laughing. But I could have died.

I'm not with that girl anymore.

14

Hafodyrynys Coal Washery, south-east Wales
The shunters may be the Gwent and the Glendower.
11 February 1973

It was so useful this place, wasn't it? Once. Gave people
a purpose. Pulled energy from the ground. Men created
wonderful mechanical answers. Then, for reasons far beyond
its control, it suddenly wasn't. It stopped being what it
was. It no longer had meaning. It became unwanted. No one
was interested anymore. Like an unloved relative in an old
person's home. They're there, but *there* isn't anywhere
meaningful. They might as well not be there.

It would probably be better for everyone if they weren't.

College Street West, Belleville, Ontario, USA
1970s

We all know how it feels to be the kid in the shadows.
Your parents want to show off their new 1970s house. Take
a picture of the neat lawn, wide drive and large,
pristine windows. To add a bit of interest on a dull day,
they need something in the foreground. They could ask you
to feature. There are a couple of nice log barriers that
you could sit on. Strike a pose. That would work. Might
even look... fun. Add a human touch to the scene. But no.
They get the dog out. Sit him down. Take his goofy
picture on this greyest of days.

And you never, ever, forget it.

"Are we staying at Disneyland, Daddy?"
"Near Disneyland."
There was a time when staying in any hotel whatsoever was a thrill. We didn't travel much when I was a kid. So when I did start exploring the wider world it took me a long time to get any perspective. A school sports trip to Jesmond in Newcastle was utterly thrilling because – my mates! – sport! – a town that wasn't my own! The fact that the B&B we stayed in should have been condemned really didn't register with me. This happy naivete lasted quite a while. It took a sewage-stained basement in Blackpool to finally shatter it. And now I have all the perspective in the world.
"I can't wait, Daddy."

Warwick Street, Heaton, Newcastle upon Tyne.
1970s

It has it all, this shot. Tower blocks, rain, a milk float, drab terraced houses, a crane, sodium street lights, a queasy sky, advertising hoardings fronting a weed-strewn wasteground. It could hardly be duller, or more 1970s. And that's even before you appreciate its most lustrous gem: the lady on the corner. Look at her. She isn't walking; both her feet are perfectly flat on the pavement. Yet she isn't talking to anyone else or even waiting for a friend's arrival – that would display a more relaxed standing position. There is tension in her stance. She has stopped abruptly and remained in that position. Transfixed. And it's the scene around her that has done this. She has turned that corner and a revelation has hit her like a Henry Cooper left hook: this is my world, and it is dull beyond fathoming.

They say that it is better to travel hopefully than to arrive. And there is a supreme joy to be found in the "setting off" part of a long or unusual journey. It's a magical mix of nervousness, hopeful anticipation and the feeling of one's own courage welling within, preparing you to embrace and conquer the Great Unknown. This always dissipates somewhat, even if your destination is an exotic place like Disneyland, Vegas, or Berwick-upon-Tweed. This begs the philosophical question – *where* does it dissipate? Can we pinpoint the moment in a journey when the "setting off" is fully over and the "disappointed arriving" has begun? We can. We have.

It is here. And now.

Inverness-shire Constabulary go "off road" during Mountain Rescue duty.
Sometime in 1973

We're in a long-wheelbase Land Rover, in a river, in the
Cairngorms… we should be having a blast, right? Of course. And
yet... and yet... this image doesn't communicate off-road
elation to me. Maybe I have Land Rover envy and that is
suppressing my joy. Tainting any potential I had for shared fun,
like the stain of spilled diesel on a concrete Esso forecourt. I
can see myself, sitting on that large rock above the bonnet,
watching the Land Rover splash by.

It passes. I sigh to myself. Open my haversack and realise that
my cheese and pickle sandwiches fell out near Glenmore Lodge.

The photographer notes that he and his pals took this shot
after shoving a broken-down Mini into Penarth dock to see how
long it would float for. This is understandable. Young warriors
growing up in a post-industrial wasteland. They were bored.
Then, one of them had the Idea. And for five glorious minutes
they were captivated, as they worked together to shove the car
into the dock – imagine the splash! – and watch it sink. Woo
hoo. What fun. But then the Mini was gone. The dock was still
wet and grey, with no promise of life or colour. And I bet
every one of those lads wished they had that broken-down Mini
back. The could have got Gareth's uncle to show them how to fix
it up. Then driven to Cardiff. Had a beer. Met some
enthusiastic valley girls. Talked about that night forever
after. But no.

29   They shoved the Mini into a dock.

Newcastle
1970s

The man with the ten thousand yard stare. She could have
the jackpot lottery ticket in her hand. Could have found
a nugget of gold. Brigitte Bardot's phone number.
Wouldn't matter to this man. He's seen the future and he
can't take his eyes off it. If she could read his mind
she'd hear the line that repeats on a loop as he sits in
this fading concrete shopping centre: "The me I think I
am does not belong here. The me I *think* I am does not
belong here. The me I think I am does *not* belong here.
The me I think I am does not belong *here*..."

This shot doesn't need much in the way of words, I
feel. The centre of London is only 50 miles away, yet
this little station is very becalmed. It would be dull
sitting on that platform, waiting for that rattly DMU.
But it would be peaceful too. Who couldn't do with more
peace in their life?

I'm going to look at this picture a little longer.

33

Is it better to walk under scaffolding or outside its area in the street? - is a question that I have thought about quite a bit. Most people prefer to walk outside it, fearing a collapse or falling debris. But, of course, a failure of the structure's integrity is unlikely to cascade vertically down; it's going to buckle like a drunk. And if one of the lads drops a hammer it's going to go out the way as well. But then my dad once told me a story about a guy who died when the scaffolding batten split clean open under his steel-toe-capped boot. He got some speed up. Crashed straight down through five levels. Strawberry jam on the pavement. However, my dad also swore blind that he'd seen the Loch Ness Monster saunter over the A82 at Drumnadrochit. Unreliable as a narrator.

Unreliable in general, now that I think about it.

The lad on the left gets it. He realises that even if he does score at the Young Farmers Ball tonight, with the prettiest girl in the county, all they can ever share together is this field of mud. This is his family farm. And, though he wants to, he hasn't the courage to be the son that breaks that tradition. It's this tractor, these furrows, this meaningless cycle of uncaring seasons... for life. His friend will get out. The professional haircut and the white jacket tell you that he's not a farmer in his soul. But what will he escape to?

37   There's mud everywhere.

Forster Square, Bradford
1974

I almost didn't include this photograph because it has fountains in it. Fountains are inherently jolly, rather than dull, I would say. Then I looked at the picture for a few more hours and realised that the fountains are in the middle of a roundabout in a busy traffic junction. And the two people sitting staring at them don't seem that impressed. Plus there is some very average concrete architecture, a washed-out sky and a sad-looking tie and shirt "gallery". The final nudge-to-include came from the lorry with a dirty skip on it.

I don't feel like its driver would be smiling as he navigated through this scene.

It's a fine building. Wilson's prize ales might be lovely.
And there's a VW Beetle in the pic, so that's always good.
But it's the chap in the hat that gets me. He's at a
literal crossroads, but also a spiritual one. He's just
staring over the junction at the town hall. Not left or
right at the traffic flow, nor at the pedestrian crossing;
there isn't one. He's eyeballing that building opposite.
Maybe the clock. Twenty to eleven. What's going down at
eleven? He knows. We don't. We never will. This is his
utterly personal moment of decision. I think he went for
it. And it wasn't pretty.

It made the lady in the bottom right-hand corner cry.

Baldwin House, St. Martins Estate, Tulse Hill,
London
Sometime in the late 1970s

I remember events like this. Sitting in your room on a gunmetal Sunday
and a shout goes up - there's a fire! So you grab a coat and scurry out
into the rain. All the boys are there, even the ones you're scared of.
But they're not interested in bullying you today, there's a greater
carnage to hold their interest. Everyone stares as real men arrive with
machines and skill, scaling the towering inferno to save lives bravely.
But the residents all got out half an hour ago. The smoke smells of old
chips. One fireman puts the fire out in thirty seconds. Then everyone
stands around for hours. After that, they leave. It's over. The only
things to see are some blackened bricks and a slightly larger puddle
than usual on the pot-holed tarmac apron in front of the flats. The big
boys are now bored. They look for you. So you run.

If only you were faster.

Ship aground on a mudbank on approach
to Cardiff docks
5 November 1972

So here we are, stuck on a mudbank on a cargo ship. The
captain's upset because he's going to get it in the neck from
the ship owners. The crew are miserable because they're not at
this moment cuddling up to ladies of negotiable virtue in
Cardiff as per their plan. And the tugboat skipper is grumpy
because he was hoping to be moored on the other side of the
river with a line over the side fishing for a nice bit of cod.
Not a fun day for anyone concerned really. Yet, someone was
there to take a photo of it. And here we are, reading about it
in a book decades later.

What on earth do we think we're *doing*?

Christmas. Santa Claus. Arriving by helicopter. That should be a
shoo-in for one of the most magical images of all time. Instead,
we have this photograph. Where there should be snow there is
muddy grass. Instead of frosted pine trees in the background
there are cranes. Standing in for the walls of the grotto are an
intimidating security fence and a dour brick building. Rather
than stepping out to a welcome party of smiling children, Santa
is being greeted by four men in flasher macs and a kid who looks
like he's going to rob the rotors off the chopper. And the big
man himself? Clearly goosed on scotch.

Ho ho ho.

"Let's remember this day out, Grandma," says her grandson, who is so proud of his new camera. And just like that, Grandma is under pressure. She thinks: "These young people think I'm past it. They hate being with me. But I treasure every second I spend with them. Must keep them interested. I know, I'll feed these cows. That will be fun. They'll like that." But the railings are broken. It's hard to reach the cows. The cows are barely interested. The young girls can't believe what is going down. They want to be in Miss Selfridge right bloody now. But Grandma can't stop. She's committed. Pulling back now would be admitting the poorness of her judgement and the width of the gulf that age creates between ourselves and our youth, and-

CLICK

-and that is how Grandma failing to feed a cow through broken railings became remembered forever.

49

York, England
Date unknown

That's probably quite an interesting historic
building, but we'll never know because the
photographer has chosen to make the main subject of
this image a large expanse of damp pavement. He or
she has also made sure to include some double yellow
lines, three truculent youths, half a 'No Parking'
sign and the back of an old lady. This cannot be
accidental. This is an image that eschews the
extraordinary for the mundane. It demands that we
wake ourselves to the banality that surrounds us and
accept it. Powerful stuff.

The tracks had been lifted here in '62, thirteen years before this shot was taken. By this time, many lines scythed by Beeching had been transformed. Built on, flattened, ploughed over. But this feels like the trains have only just gone. Just pop the rails back and they'll be here again in a jiff. If only. What breaks my heart about Britain's vanished railway lines isn't the loss of metal, engine and road. It's the fact that a generation of leaders felt fine about taking away *places to go to*. Our little country is small enough. And they made it smaller. With a snort, a nod and the stroke of a pen.

53   Nice Landy, mind.

Windsor Road, Penarth, Wales
5 February 1973

Closing. Down. Sale. Are there three more depressing words? At first
when you see them there's a little fillip to your greed centre: "I
could bag a bargain!" But that is soon displaced by the judder of
loss. Even if you never shopped there anyway that was because you
chose not to. Now that control has been taken from you. A closed
door. Lost opportunity. Another path untaken. Maybe Vennings was
where Happiness lay for you. It was sitting there on a shelf. All you
had to do was go in, pick it up and put your money down. You could
have held it all in your hands. But now you'll never know.

Meanwhile, the shopkeeper is slumped by the till, grinding away the
tears with his fists: "Why don't they like me? They don't even come
in for cheap Happiness."

Remember when arcades were classy? Or at least interesting? I can picture myself running down those covered, echoing, rain-free streets to browse in record shops, stationers, hardware merchants, model shops, tool stores, even saddlers. There was so much to see. Now the one near where I live is all tourist tat and kebab shops.

I guess there's more call for chicken donners than martingales these days but my soul wishes that weren't the case.

"Be patient, it's just round the next bend... wait... no, not this
bit... calm down, it's only a little further... not far, trust me...
and... Yes! Here. The perfect spot for a picnic - don't you think so
my dear?"

Picnics are a great notion: eating fine food on a glorious day in the
great outdoors with your loved ones. But it only takes one of those
components to fail and the whole enterprise veers into a ditch. And
one of them ALWAYS does. The food is limp ham sandwiches and oily
dips. The outdoors is either rammed or dismal. Your loved ones are
hateful. And, of course, our weather is so wonderfully modest with her
glories. Picnics are a powerful metaphor for much in life.

God bless the dog, though. He's happy. Poor sod.

Most jobs hold no glamorous promise. You know if you work in a
chicken factory that there isn't a more exciting chicken factory
somewhere else that you could be working in. It is what it is.
The work may be dull, but you don't need to worry that you're
missing out. You can accept the dullness. But here the
disappointment must have burned in the soul like lava. This
officer could have gone home and watched Michael Douglas ripping
it up in the Streets of San Francisco. Gasped at Starsky and
Hutch gunning their red Gran Torino round Bay City. Rolled
through LA with swinging Jim Rockford. That's what being a
detective could be like. But not here. Not for me.

Who loves ya, baby?

61   Probably no one.

Ossulton Way, London
Sometime in 1976

What *is* the sound of the suburbs? Bluebottles buzzing in endless loops on the landing... the distant moan of traffic on the bypass... siblings whining at your mother downstairs... the dog three doors down yelping at the one-legged pigeon that taunts him... the receding echo of your Hopes and Dreams as they march arm and arm over the TV-aerial-dotted horizon... But then, from the direction of the station comes the "Clack-Click-Clack" of glamorous shoes. This is remarkable! Alien. Strange. Thrilling. Grab your camera. To immortalise this magical moment. And... there she is!

GLORY!

But then she's gone. And you have to wait another lifetime to get the photos back from Boots.

Still. The 1976 Citroen GS is very nice.

This special shot was taken from the photographer's
window. I wish this had been the view from my bedroom
window when I was growing up. All I could see through my
iron-barred panes was a stone wall about six feet away
across a muddy, junk-strewn yard. That was pleasingly
bleak, don't get me wrong, but there was no *scale* to the
vista's grimness. And scale can make all the difference;
I had nothing to compare myself with.

But to look out through the sleet at these steel works
lurking at the bottom of a scrubby hill... well that
puts some spectacular perspective on the evanescence of
your own existence.

Station Road, South Gosforth
1970s

Sometimes I like to lighten the mood with an image that shows the indefatigable human spirit fighting the dullness around them. The elderly lady on the left is fully acceptant of the profoundly bleak scene around her. She's just crossing that wet, pot-holed road as fast as she can to get to a place she hopes will be less dull than this one but knows in her heart won't be. Her companion, however, has spotted the photographer and is attempting to do something amusing — a skip, or a favourite dance step from her vanished youth. I admire her courage while at the same time fearing for her balance.

It's almost a certainty that seconds after the shutter closed on this scene, she fell over. Cracked a hip, I bet.

That's New Scotland Yard we're looking into. Which
makes it almost interesting, I suppose. We can say with
certainty that important events have occurred and
decisions of great moment been taken within these
walls. But not today. There's nothing happening today.
There isn't even anyone on their way to get a cup of
tea at the Barclay Bros café. Also, it's slightly
depressing that only the "IN" gate is open. This is a
blatant and dark piece of intimidation: "you can enter
but you'll never leave". It's like Life really. No one
ever gets out. I mean, you could make a case for
Beyoncé.

But I doubt that even she is free of that which one
should pity her for.

She was a lovely lady I'm sure. Loved her family no doubt, and was loved by them. So why does this photograph of a happy memory make me feel so... suicidal? Because I remember so many days like this, visiting my own Granny, who lived in a place like that. The terrifying food. The cat-infused furnishings. The mountainous boredom. You know, I hear people say to kids these days: "You don't know you're born. You have so much more that we had as kids." And they're dead right. There's no way that kids today are ever as bored as we were then. The highlight - the absolute highlight - of Sundays at Granny's was when you could stop poking the mutton fat and cabbage around your plate and go over to sit on the spring-filled sofa to watch Songs of Praise and Last of The Summer Wine. That was the high point kids, believe me.

The best it ever got.

There's a very particular moment in life that comes to most of us. I remember it hit me when I was twelve and I was walking down the steps that led to the school gym hall. The doors were swinging in front of me and I got a waft of unwashed kids and the thought crashed into my brain like Evil Knievel on benzedrine: "I'm going to die." I'd thought many times before about the fact that all people do die. And I was aware that I was a person. Yet I hadn't put those thoughts together logically. Until that moment. When I understood. Yes, I really am leaving this place sometime. Swapping everything for nothing. Becoming vacuum. And that's what's happening here. This lad isn't swithering over which vol au vent to have, or looking at a pretty waitress. He's in the middle of a psychic rupture that will reframe every action, desire and hope that was ever his as utterly meaningless.

73 And the moustache? No, my friend, not even that will save your soul.

Penguins at Edinburgh Zoo
20 July 1972

Who's in captivity here? Sure, the penguins can't hot-
flipper it to Antarctica if they fancy it, but at least they
are doing what's in their nature. Mucking about in the
water. Eating fish. Not flying. But are we doing what's in
our nature, when we go to the zoo? Well, if we were destined
by the mighty engine of evolution to spend a whole day
watching pandas not come out of doors, monkeys fiddle with
their bits and polar bears weave their heads from side to
side in silent madness all while trying to interest
fractious children in the scene after paying a fortune for
the privilege and later having to deal with the vagaries of
the number 26 bus then YES! It's in our nature.

But the penguins must think we are dumb beasts.

Blackett Street, Newcastle upon Tyne
1970s - exact date unknown but
maybe a Friday night

You think you know what's going on in this picture: the young
"faces" are overtaking the slow-moving older woman on their way
to the flicks. Or to buy the Quadrophenia LP. There's a happy
couple behind and some people queueing for a bus in the rain. But
do you really know for sure? What if that lady and the lad who's
finishing picking his nose had just met up on a blind date? He
took his sandy-haired best mate with him because he was nervous.
Now he's even more scared because he's only ever been with silly
lasses, and his date has turned out to be a mature, wise woman
who brooks no nonsense. And *she's* hacked off because she was
expecting more of a MAN. Someone like Kris Kristofferson. For
once, her fatalistic expression is nothing to do with the rain or
failed ambition or the concrete prison around her.

77   It's the fact that her blind date is a wimp.

Portree Harbour, Isle of Skye, Scotland
Date unknown

Sea eagles nest on those cliffs in the background. The
quayside is usually buzzing with boats and fishermen.
Seals lark about in the water, turning tricks for scraps.
Cosy pubs beckon from the harbourside. The finest
mountains in Britain are just off to the right. And I do
understand that this photograph was taken of a loved one,
to remember a moment shared. Of course. But it reminds me
so much of the photos I took, or were taken of me, where
my family, or I, were the ones in the shot and we didn't
see any of the eagles, mountains, seals or exciting pubs
either. Just got out of the car, stood front and centre
of the wondrous scene, clicked the shutter, got back in
the blinking car. Oh, to be able to look around!

Like in Blade Runner.

Not much of a religious chap myself but, generally, if
people find peace in going to church, what does it bother
me? Well, it might bother me if they found peace in going
to this church, on a day like today. That might suggest a
certain masochistic streak in one's character. Trouble in
the soul. Furious jealousy suppressed only by the weight
of stacked hymn books.

If I were a police detective in this locality and a
citizen came in to complain that someone had yelled at a
bunch of kids for having a harmless kickabout in the
park, I know where I'd start my enquiries.

Victoria Embankment, London
Date unknown

You join the action in the middle of a pavement artist
contest. The judges will have their work cut out. The
standard appears on the low side. I like art, don't get
me wrong, and I respect the effort here. I just feel
awfully sorry for these poor sods. I mean, at what point
do you think, "I know, I will make my art where people
can stand on it, dogs can dump on it and the rain will
wash it away by the weekend." If you're bad at art, fair
enough, your embarrassment won't be around for long. But
if you're any good it must be terribly bleak: I create,
they stare blankly, it all fades.

That's careers for you.

Life was so dull in the 1970s that seeing even the most lowly of local celebrities was a moment of note. And it's so depressing. All this guy did was read the news – for a short time – on a regional magazine TV show and here he is in his 'Frisco shades, white suit and chunky rings, opening some new centre and thinking he's the king of us all. Just the way he's holding that microphone is grounds for murder. That sounds bitter, I know. Maybe he was a decent bloke. It's just... once when I was a kid I was sitting in the hairdressers waiting my turn when my mum says, "That's Nick off that TV show. You know, the fun one." I didn't know who she meant or which TV show she was talking about. But the fact that she was impressed made me feel like I had to respond in an appropriate way. Which was? Ask the guy for his autograph. So I ended up taking a paper tissue over to a grown man I didn't know who was having his hair washed and asking him to sign it. I felt ashamed then and I cringe now.

85   Banality infects like a disease and there is no cure.

I had thought of doing a book called "Dull Days Of The 1970s Up Alleys". It proved a little too niche. Couldn't source enough images. Well, I found images but I discovered that they weren't of what are locally called alleys. There are a great many dialect terms that are technically correct and should be used instead: ginnel, snicket, jinny, vennel, twitten, pend, and what we have here: a close. That's the old Edinburgh word for a narrow alley. Maybe I'll do a book called "Dull Days Of The 1970s Up Edinburgh Closes".

Marketing is hard.

Morris Marina by the Four Crosses pub
at the junction with the A34 and
Leamore Lane. Walsall
Late 1970s

Almost exciting, but... not really. The police driver is doing his rounds, ready for action. But there are no bad guys to chase. No lost tourists. No truanting boys. None of the neighbourhood cats are stuck up any of the neighbourhood trees. This will be a long shift. Then he spots the photographer! The man's squinting into his camera's viewfinder. He's adjusting the focus, ready to shoot... the officer plants his foot, slings the squad car wide into the roundabout, then pulls the wheel hard right, gunning for the exit - this is going to look just like Bullitt.

But the car is slow and heavy, it corners like the Ark Royal, and... here we are.

**The Old Weavers House on the
River Stour, Canterbury
August 1973**

Here's a dull day in the 1570s.

Just my little joke there. The quip was based on the fact that
these buildings in Canterbury look like they're from the Tudor
period, which ran from 1485 to 1603. Of course, photography
wasn't invented until 1839 so it doesn't really work as a joke.
Plus I've explained it now, which those in the know say you
should never do with humour. I'm not much of a comedian.
Although, pleasingly, it does make me realise that I have
something in common with many of the Old Masters. Hay carts
stuck in rivers, soldiers sat on horses, a couple called Andrews
stood under a tree, thirteen folk eating supper - those artists
chose some awfully dull days to capture in their paintings.

Interesting place, Cardiff. Looks like there's a proper medieval castle just sat next to the shops and pubs. But it's a bit tricksy. The castle on show today was mostly created by the 3rd Marquess of Bute in the 19th century. He was the richest man in the world. An orphan, though. Bit like a Welsh batman, I suppose. Six days after this shot was taken these streets were thronging with rugby fans as Wales beat England 20-4 on their way to winning the Five Nations. The Welsh used to piss in my garden on match day. Red ranks of them would just step over the wall, line up and let loose on my roses.

By that time I couldn't stop them.

"I thought it would somehow be *more* than this," the chap with the beard is thinking. "Surely whipping round Trafalgar square sitting high on the body of a vintage fire engine would be... exciting... eye-catching... unforgettable... and it's sort of fun, but it wasn't what I'd hoped when Bob mentioned the idea. It seemed like such a lark then. But it's cold. Draughty. You notice how much gunk car exhausts really pump out when you're al fresco in traffic. And people are just sort of staring at us. Not in admiration or envy. They're thinking: 'I bet they thought it would be more fun than this.' And they're right. Because is there *anything* in Life that's as fun as you think it will be?"

You're asking the wrong man, my friend.

Till death us do part, they say. More like till life us do part, if you ask me. The quotidian responsibilities, self-replicating tasks and vanishing desires of ordinary existence push people apart remorselessly. We are joined at the altar in a locus of perfect unity. But thereafter - in fact, the very moment that the union is completed - reality inserts the tip of its wedge between us. The universe then uses all its infinite might to drive that wedge down further every day. Spreading, splitting, dividing, driving hearts further apart.

See, it has started here already for this confetti-strewn man and his faceless belle.

97

Grainger Market, Newcastle upon Tyne
1970s

Yes my friend, this is your life: you're second fiddle on
a tripe stall. Now please believe me, I'm not saying that
to be mean. I've been third fiddle in a cleaning company,
seventeenth fiddle in a call centre and the guy the whole
warehouse (even smelly wee June who worked the compactor)
slagged off in a warehouse. Duff jobs, I know about.
Phoney managers lording it over you in those duff jobs,
ditto with bells on. I'm saying that because this image
so perfectly captures the moment that the dullness of the
days ahead hit this man.

Like a forpit of tripe in his face.

I have presented these photographs as a triptych because I think they work as complementary fragments of a whole scene. And it's a scene that raises many questions on multiple layers. How intense is this rug? Why pick *that* pattern for the sofa? What does the kitten think it's doing? Whose glasses are those? Why are they so odd-looking? Is the kitten going to chew them? Put them on? Why does the kitten look wise beyond its years? Where are its siblings? How lonely does it feel? We don't know.

One thing we do know: this kitten is dead now.

Sealink Ferry "INVICTA" shortly before decommissioning and scrapping, Newhaven, England
1972

Off to France on the ferry. This will be fun. Fine food and drink. Culture. Stylish people. Perhaps a nice cathedral. It will all be different then. The start of a new chapter. A brighter reality. You can taste the fresh tang of hope in the salty air. Everyone on the boat feels it; optimism is infectious. On arrival you're bobbing from foot to foot as you queue by the gangway door. Metal clanks, winches hum. The sun cracks open the sky. And here we go. Time to step out into a new land...

Yet, no matter how far you travel, no matter how glamorous your destination, the first thing you encounter when you get there is the same old you.

ACKNOWLEDGEMENTS

We are grateful to the following individuals and organisations for making the images on the noted pages available under Creative Commons Licence 2.0 (unless otherwise indicated thus [...]): 8, 19 Flickr user Community Archives [Public Domain]; 11, 23, 31, 56, 67, 76, 99 Flickr user Newcastle Libraries [Public Domain]; 12 Flickr user bestgiftsphotos; 15 Flickr user Roger W Haworth; 16, 28, 44, 52, 55, 92 Flickr user Ben Salter [Public Domain]; 20 Flickr user Dunedin City Council Archives; 24 Flickr user Rob Russell; 27, 60 Flickr user Dave Conner; 32 Flickr user 70023venus2009; 35, 48, 51, 59, 71, 79, 96, 100 Flickr user foundin_a_attic; 36 Flickr user Teddy Ruxpin2; 39 Flickr user shipley43; 40 Flickr user Andrew Huddart; 43, 68, 83, 95 Flickr user Leonard Bentley; 47 Flickr user City of Boston Archives; 63 Flickr user David Howard; 64 Flickr user Robin Taylor; 72 Flickr user Ed Uthman; 75 Flickr user alljengi; 80 Flickr user Michelle O'Connell; 84 Flickr user Tony oldroyd; 87 Flickr user stu smith; 88 Flickr user West Midlands Police; 91 Flickr user reivax; 103 Flickr user Barry Lewis.

COMING SOON

Dull Days Of The 1960s

Nigel Norman

Dull Days Of The 1980s

Nigel Norman

If you like your boredom in a different vintange you can pre-order these titles at www.dull-days.com. I'm working on them at the moment and should have them finished soon.

I'll bet you can hardly wait.

Nigel Norman
September 2018

Printed in Great Britain
by Amazon